Tunisia

Complete and Easy Guide To Awesome

Tunisian Crochet Patterns and Projects

Table of Contents

Introduction

There you are, in another craft fair, admiring every little trinket the artists have worked so hard putting together. It is very true that each piece is a work of art, and you are definitely impressed time and time again as you see each and every piece.

Then you see the fiber arts. There is just something magical about these crafts, as they are all made of different kinds of patterns and fibers, and stitches! How do they make those stitches anyway? Some are small and compact, others are loose and draping, but whatever they are doing, they are all breath taking.

When you are able to make these things yourself, you are going to see how much time and effort goes into each one, and it is going to take on a whole new meaning when you walk through the art fair and see all the different projects people have made.

There is no end to the ways you can make things, and how many pieces you can design out of your own mind. This book is going to show you exactly how you can take your projects from the level of regular crochet, to the advanced level of Tunisian crochet.

It doesn't matter if you know crochet or not, although it does help if you do, as we will show you exactly what you need to know to get your project up and running. All you need is a little bit of enthusiasm, and a willingness to learn, and you are going to find that you have what it takes to make your own Tunisian crochet projects.

Let your imagination soar, as that is the best way to open your mind to creativity. Each and every pattern you see online is one that had to be invented at one point in time, and the next best seller can be created by you.

All you need to do is let your creative side out, and embrace all you have to give, and you will see that anyone can make beautiful crafts that are worthy of blue ribbons every day of the week.

So what you are waiting for? Brew yourself a nice cup of tea, grab your favorite ball of yarn, and get out your specialty crochet hooks, you are about to discover a new and beautiful craft that you can pass on to those around you, and show the world what you have to offer!

Chapter 1 – All about Tunisian Crochet

Getting Started With Tunisian Crochet

If you've worked with crocheting, or know the basics, you'll have an easier time picking up Tunisian crochet. Crocheting begins with a foundation chain and so does Tunisian crochet. With the Tunisian version you need to make a whole foundation row with a forward and return pass. The foundation row is almost always the same style too no matter what pattern or stich you use. It's all about what you do after that basic stitch.

To get started with Tunisian crochet you need to start with a slip knot and a chain stitch. To practice working your basic foundation row make a chain stitch of fifteen chains and go from there. The chain needs to be the same length as the amount of stitches you're going to work with. For example if you're working with ten stitches then your chain needs to be ten chains long. Fifteen is a basic and easy number to work with so use that as your practice.

To start working with your foundation row and working the forward pass start by inserting your hook into the second chain from the hook. That's how things work in regular crocheting too. You almost always ignore the first chain from the hook.

After inserting the hook into the chain you yarn over, which is pulling the yarn over the hook, and then pull up the loop you've made. After that you should have two loops on your hook.

You need to keep the loops on the hook at all times. You also need to repeat this step for every chain on the hook. So by the time that you've finished you should have fifteen loops on your hook. That's another major difference between crochet and Tunisian crochet. You keep the loops on the hook. That's why the Tunisian crochet hook is so much longer.

Now it's time to work on the return pass of your foundation row. The return pass goes from left to right. Remember to not turn your work. You're doing this so that you don't have to turn anything over. To start the return pass begin by yarning over, and then pull through the first loop. Then you yarn over again and this time pull through two loops. This is the process you repeat for the rest of the row. You go through two loops at a time for the return pass and stop when you have one loop left. That's your first foundation row down!

This is when you start the first row. What you're working on now is actually a very basic swatch pattern that has you repeat the first row. So when you're done with this row just repeat it until you're satisfied.

Row one has vertical bars that are created from the foundation row. Remember to count them to make sure that you have the same number of bars as you do stitches. You also need to remember to use the last bar at the end.

To start the first rows forward pass skip the first vertical bar and insert your hook into the second one. Yarn over and pull up a loop to get two loops on your hook. Keep up that pattern until you go through every bar and have fifteen loops on your hook.

Now it's time to work the return pass. Yarn over and pull through the first loop. You'll only pull through the first loop at the beginning of the return pass. Then you yarn over and pull through two loops. Keep doing that until you have only one loop left, as you did before. Then you have another fifteen vertical bars. Just keep doing that until you're happy with the size of the swatch.

There's one very simple pattern down and one crucial skill learned. Let's now take a look at some others.

Crochet Master List

Abbreviation	Directions	Abbreviation	Directions
[ ]	Complete the instructions inside the brackets the number of times indicated	FPdc	Front post and double crochet
( )	Complete the instructions inside the parentheses the number of times indicated	FPsc	Front post single crochet
*	Repeat the instructions after the asterisk the number of times indicated	FPtc	Front post double crochet
**	Repeat the instructions between the asterisks the number of times indicated	G	Gram
"	Inches	hdc	Half double crochet
Alt	Alternate	inc	Increase
Approx	Approximately	lp	Loop
Beg	Beginning	m	Meter

Bet	Between	MC	Main Color
BL	Back Loop	mm	Millimeter
Bo	Bobble	oz	Ounces
BP	Back Post	p	Pico
BPdc	Back post double crochet	pat	Pattern
BPsc	Back post single crochet	pc	Popcorn
BPtc	Back post treble crochet	pm	Place Marker
CA	Color A	prev	Previous
CB	Color B	rem	Remaining
CC	Coordinating Color	rep	Repeat
ch	Chain Stitch	rnd	Rounds
ch-	Previous chain stitch	RS	Right Side
ch-sp	Chain Space	sc	Single Crochet
CL	Cluster	sc2tog	Single crochet 2 together
cm	Centimeter	sk	Skip
cont	Continue	Slst	Slip stitch
dc	Double Crochet	sp	Space

dc2tog	Double crochet two stitches together	st	Stitch
dec	Decrease	Tch or t-ch	Turn stitch
dtr	Double Treble	tbl	Through the back loop
FL	Front Loop	tog	Together
Foll	Follow	tr	Treble crochet
FP	Front Post	trtr	Triple treble crochet
		WS	Wrong side
		yd	Yard
		yo	Yarn over
		yoh	Yarn over hook
		Tss	Tunisian Simple Stitch
		Tks	Tunisian Knit Stitch

Advanced Techniques

As easy as Tunisian crochet is it isn't all just simple stitches and foundation rows. There are other things you need to know. One skill you definitely need to know is how to finish your work when you're done.

When the time comes to finish your work you start by completing the return pass on the last row of the pattern. You can fasten off similar to what you do in regular crochet, which is tightening everything up and then cutting the yarn, or you can do something fun by making a neater edge using slip stitches. To make a neater edge insert the hook under second vertical strand, bypassing the outside edge.

Pull the yarn through both loops of the hook and repeat that action along the row and you'll have made a neat little slip stitch to give your product a more polished look. It looks a lot better than just fastening off and makes the pattern a little more unique.

Another little advanced trick to know how to do is switching colors. Changing the color is needed in some patterns. You can also use it on a single color pattern to add some stripes for a bit of colorful flair. You can also use this technique to switch yarn if you find yourself running out. Whether you want to change colors or switch to a different ball of yarn here is the technique for how to do it.

If you're changing color to create solid stripes in your pattern then you need to change for the start of the forward pass. That means you pick up the new color at the end of the last reverse pass. Just hook in the new color at the end, as you would do with regular crochet. Fit it through the loop and you'll have yourself two solid blocks of color. That's also how you swap yarn of the same color. You'll have two solid blocks of the same color so no one will be able to tell that you switched yarn.

There's another little trick you can do when it comes to swapping colors. You could create two solid blocks of color, and there's nothing wrong with that, but what if you wanted to do something a little more? If you change color at the beginning of the reverse pass, rather than the end, you get an entirely different effect. All you have to do is work the forward pass in the old color, then pick up your new color at the start of the chain in the reverse pass. This makes the old color sort of fold over the new color and create an almost tunnel like effect that helps avoid some issues with the way the color stripes look, as well as adding a unique flair to your project.

There plenty of other little things you can do to add some fun to your project. There's one last one that we'll look at before moving on to some patterns for you to try. The last little advanced thing to show you is how to make a cross stitch.

Begin by chaining an odd number of chains for your foundation row. We recommend seventeen but any odd number will do. You might want to stick to the basic fifteen you've been doing until now. Remember the foundation row will almost always be the same so you don't need us to tell you how to do that again.

To start with the cross stitch skip the first and second vertical bars of your forward pass and instead insert the hook into the third bar. Then you yarn over and pull up a loop, giving you two loops on your hook.

Now, and this is where it gets a little complicated, you need to work into the second bar that you just skipped. That's why you skipped it. There's no need to turn your work or do anything fancy. Just bring the hook back and insert it into the second bar. Yarn over and pull up a loop, giving you three loops on your hook. You should be able to see already that you've made an ever so tiny cross stitch.

You just need to do that all the way across, like you did for the basic stitch. Remember to skip one bar and work on the one after, and then go back through the bar you skipped. That gets the stitches to cross over.

Now it's time to work the return pass. Work from left to right, as you always do on the return, and yarn over and pull through the first loop on the hook. For the rest of the pass you yarn over and pull through two loops, as you did before. Then you just repeat row one until you get the amount of rows you need. After a few rows you'll be able to really see the cross pattern and how great it looks.

Now that you know the basics of how to do Tunisian crochet it's time to take a look at some actual patterns for you to try at home. We're focusing on kid friendly ones. You might even want to teach your kids how to do some Tunisian crochet to give them a hobby. The length of the hooks might make it a little tricky for a small child to pick up but they can definitely give it a good go with a little help.

Tunisian Simple Stitch – Tss/TSS

Insert hook into second stitch from the hook

Yarn over/Yo

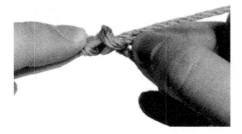

Pull the yarn through one loop on the hook so there is one loop on the hook

Insert the hook into the next stitch

Yo and pull through one loop on the hook now there is one loop on the hook

Continue with Yo and pull through first loop on the hook until the number of loops on the hook is the same as the number of stitches used in the original chain

Yo and pull through the first stitch/loop on the hook

Yo and pull through the next two loops on the hook

Continue alternating between one and two loops until the end is reached

One finished row of the Tunisian Simple Stitch

Tunisian Knit Stitch – Tks/TKS

The Tunisian knit stitch differs from the simple stitch because the hook is inserted under the vertical bars or the stitches, not through. Create the first row of Tunisian simple stitch then on each forward pass insert the hook under the vertical stitches, Yo and pull through. The return pass is the same as the return pass in the simple stitch, Yo and pull through the first loop on the hook, then insert the hook Yo and pull through the next two loops on the hook.

Chapter 2 – Projects for Kids

Wrist Warmers

We'll start with something every kid needs at some point; wrist warmers. These wrist warmers should end up being about six and a half inches long and two inches tall.

The materials you're going to need for this pattern are three different colors of medium weight yarn, a 5.5mm Tunisian crochet hook, a yarn needle, and a pair of scissors.

The gauge isn't very important with this pattern but to give you an idea 7 rows should be about 2 inches thick. The pattern makes two of the warmers, or enough for one kid, and is laid out below.

Row 1: Start by chaining ten with your first color. If you chain ten and it doesn't look tall enough you can chain a few more. Just remember to chain the same amount further down the line. Change to the second color in the last chain and simple stitch starting from the second chain from the hook, then in each chain across. Change to the third color at the beginning of the reverse pass, then change back to the first color in the last simple stitch of the reverse pass.

Row 2: Simple stitch in the second stitch from the hook and in each stitch across. Switch to your second color at the start of the reverse pass. Then switch to your third color at the last simple stitch of the reverse pass.

Row 3: Simple stitch in the second stitch from the hook and in each stitch across. Switch to your first color at the start of the reverse pass. Then switch to your second color at the last simple stitch of the reverse pass.

Row 4: Simple stitch in the second stitch from the hook and in each stitch across. Switch to your third color at the start of the reverse pass. Then switch to your first color at the last simple stitch of the reverse pass.

After that you need to repeat rows 2-4 seven more times at the least. Or just keep going until the wrist warmer is large enough for you. Then move on to row five.

Row 5: Slip stitch in the second stitch from the hook and in each stitch across. All you have to do after that is just finish off.

To make your button you need to use this pattern:

Round 1: Chain two then five sc in the second chain from the hook.

Round 2: Use 4 sc in the same chain, overlapping your previous round. Then finish off.

The strap is pretty easy. To do that you just have to chain six and then finish off.

To finish off the wrist warmers properly sew a button to one end of the wrist warmer and then sew the strap to the opposite end.

Baby Blanket

Use baby soft yarn, blue for a boy and pink for a girl.

This pattern is much like the basic blankets that we have made in the last chapter. The point of this pattern is for you to get used to the different texture of the different yarns, and learn how to work with different kinds of fibers.

Cast on 50, then Tunisian crochet across the row. Chain 1, turn, and single crochet back across the other side. Repeat this until you are happy with the length of the blanket.

Tie off securely, babies are wiggly and you don't want them to get their fingers stuck in any loose threads!

Perfect Pillows

2 skeins of acrylic yarn in the color of your choice.

Cast on 25. Single crochet across the row, then chain 1 and turn. Repeat this until you have a square, and tie off. Make another square patch the same size as the first, and tie off.

Next, using a yarn needle, sew the two squares together, leaving a little side open for the stuffing. Turn the right way, stuff the pillows until they are plump, and sew the opening shut. Add a nice fringe border to make them look flirty.

Miniature Hat Ornament

This great little hat is the ideal decoration for a Christmas tree, or just a wonderful little project for you to have a go at. The finished size of the hat is about 1 and three quarter inches across and high.

You're going to need nine yards of worsted weight yarn, an I hook (that's 5.5mm) and a yarn needle. The gauge should be about four stitches for an inch but gauge isn't overly important here.

Here's the pattern:

Row 1: Chain sixteen and then skip the first chain. Pull up the loop through the back bump of each stitch so you have sixteen loops on your hook. Then yarn over and pull through one loop. Yarn over then pull through two loops and repeat that until only one loop is left.

Rows 2-8: Skip the first vertical bar. Insert the hook from the front to the back between strands of the next vertical bar. Yarn over and then pull up a loop. Repeat that across. To return you yarn over and pull through one loop. Then yarn over and pull through two loops until one loop is left.

Row 9: Skip the first vertical bar then insert the hook from the front to the back between strands of the next vertical bar. You yarn over, and pull up a loop, then repeat that across. To return just yarn over and pull the loop through all the other loops in the row, going one or two at a time. That's how you gather the crown of the hat. Finish off and then pull tight.

To finish you turn so the wrong side is facing and whipstitch the vertical edge closed. If you've done it right the bottom edge should flip up naturally. Secure the yarn to the inside of the crown and turn the right side out, and make a loop about three inches high. Knot the yarn near the crown, secure the yarn inside of the hat, and weave in all the ends. There you have it; one tiny little hat.

Tunisian Scarf

One common item that's made with crocheting is a scarf. Here's a look at just one of the many kinds of scarves you can make with Tunisian crocheting. Or, indeed, any kind of crocheting.

You're going to need 7 skeins of wool and a size J (6 mm) Afghan crochet hook. Remember Afghan crochet is just another way of saying Tunisian crochet. The gauge is that 14 stitches comes to about 4 inches.

To get started you need to work your foundation chain. For this pattern you need to chain 42 stitches. When you've made your foundation it's time to work with row 1.

Forward Row 1: Insert your hook through the space between the vertical strands, then yarn over and pull a loop through the hook. Insert the hook into the next space, yarn over, and pull the loop through onto the hook. Repeat that until you get to the last space, which needs to be skipped. Instead you insert your Afghan hook into the chain stitch at the edge. Pull the loop through onto the hook.

Return row 1: Chain one stitch, yarn over, and pull the loop through the next two stitches on the hook. Repeat until you get to the end, ending with one loop on the hook.

Forward row 2: Insert the hook into the second space, yarn over, and pull the loop through onto the hook. Insert the hook into the third space, yarn over, and pull the loop through onto the hook. Repeat that to the end of the row, including the last space. Insert your Afghan hook into the chain stitch at the edge, pull the loop through onto the hook.

Return row 2: Just do the same thing you did for the first return row. Then you just repeat these steps until the scarf is as long as you want it. The original pattern calls for 70 inches but that's way too long for a kid.

Now it's time for the finish.

This time when you do the first forward row insert the hook into the first space, yarn over, and pull through two loops on the hook. Repeat this until the end when you should have one loop left on the hook. Then you cut the yarn and pull through the remaining loop.

With the right side facing you, as you should for Tunisian crochet, join the yarn and make a single crochet into each stitch along the edge you're going to bind off. Cut the yarn and pull through the remaining loop. Repeat that for the cast-on edge and then weave in all the ends and block how you want to finish completely.

Faux Knit Headband

This headband is great for keeping your kids heads warm and it's as soft as it looks.

You need two colorways of worsted weight yarn, a size J Tunisian crochet hook, and a yarn needle. Safety pins will help but aren't necessary. There isn't much of a gauge in this pattern either. Just keep going until it's the right size. You want to make one that's a few inches short because the yarn does stretch.

To begin with make a foundation chain nine stitches long using your first color.

Row 1: Work your forward pass in the first color. Drop the first color at the end and work your way back using the second color.

Row 2: Work the forward pass in the second color. Drop the second color at the end and work your way back using the first color.

Just repeat that until the headband is as long as you need it to be. When you finish the last row use a slip stitch in each stitch across.

When the headband is the right size it's time to finish it up. Cut the yarn, but leave a long trail of about ten inches long. Thread your yarn needle (you can also use a tapestry needle for this step) and stitch the two ends together. Weave in the ends and turn the headband right side out and you're good to go.

Row 4: Skip first vertical bar. Working as for a Tunisian full stitch, insert the hook under the first horizontal bar and pull up a loop. Still working as for a Tunisian full stitch, insert hook under the next 16 horizontal bars, pulling up loops for each. Close the same as before.

Row 5: Skip first horizontal and vertical bars. Working as for Tunisian full stitch, insert hook under the remaining horizontal bars, even the ones from row 2-4. Pull up loops in each one too. Working as for Tunisian knot stitch, pull up a loop in the last vertical bar, giving you 38 loops on the hook. Close by yarning over and pull through one loop on the hook 7 times. Yarn over and pull through 3 loops on the hook 8 times. Yarn over and pull through 3 loops on hook. Yarn over and pull through two loops repeatedly until done.

Bind off by skipping the first vertical bar. Then, working for TFS, slip under each horizontal bar across. Then cut off the remaining yarn. With the yarn needle and about 18 inches of yarn seam the last row to the foundation row. Weave the yarn loosely along the edges of each row at the top of your hat using a different piece of yarn. Cinch gently to draw the hole together and sew it together to maintain the closure. Weave all the ends in securely and flip the hat "inside out" to finish.

Tunisian Crochet Cellphone Bag

Do your children have cell phones? If they do you can use this design to create a handy little bag for them to keep it in.

You need some size ten cotton thread in green and greensh grey. Or just two colors that fit well together. A 3.5 mm steel crochet hook. A sea shell bead, and some Velcro fastening finish the list.

To make the body use a double strand of green to chain 18 + 2. Use a basic Tunisian stitch on these 18 chains for 44 rows. Then fasten up.

The flap is a little more complicated. Join a double strand of greenish grey at the beginning of the last row and work on sc in each stitch across. Then turn.

Row 2: chain three, dec over next two sc, 1 sc in each sc across to the last sc. Then dec over the last two and turn.

Row 3: Chain 2, 1 sc in each sc across to the end. Turn.

Then you repeat row 2 and 3 until 2 sc remain. Pass the thread through both and fasten off.

For the strap you knit an I-cord using one strand of green and one strand of grey. You do this by using a pair of double pointed 3mm needles, cast on 3 stitches. Knit across. Slide the stitches across the needle to the right edge and, bringing the thread to the right and behind the work, knit across again. Keep that up until the strap is as long as it needs to be and cast off the three stitches together to finish.

Finish the bag properly by sewing the sides together by using a weave stitch. Use the grey to crochet a row of sc along the margins of the flap. Attach the seashell bead to the top of the flap. Then sew the I-cord and Velcro fastening in place.

Tunisian Stitch Neck Warmer

This great little neck warmer is idea for keeping your loved ones necks warm in the cold weather.

You need two colors of medium weight yarn, a size I crochet hook, a yarn needle, and a pair of scissors. The gauge is that 7 rows should equal 2 inches.

Use the green yarn to chain 20, or as wide as you'd like the neck warmer to be.

Row 1: Work a simple stitch in the second chain from the hook, and in each chain across.

Row 2-53: Work the simple stitch in the second stitch and in each stitch across

Row 54: Work a simple stitch in the second stitch and in each stitch across. This time change to brown yarn in the last simple stitch.

Row 55-74: Work a simple stitch in the second stitch and then each stitch across.

Row 75: Work a slip stitch in the second stitch and then in each stitch across. Finish off.

To make the button (and you need to make two) just follow this pattern.

Row 1: Use the green yarn to chain 4, slip stitch in the forth chain from the hook to form a loop.

Row 2: Work ten sc in the loop.

Row 3: Work ten sc in the loop, overlapping the previous row.

Row 4: Work eight sc in the loop, overlapping the previous one again, and finish off.

To make the button strap, and again you need to make 2, use this pattern.

Row 1: Chain 15, then slip stitch in the first chain to form a loop, then finish off.

Use a yarn needle to sew the buttons onto the brown end of the neck warmer, and the button straps onto the green end.

Afghan Stitch Coaster

It's a small thing but a coaster can go a long way and makes for a fun small project and handmade gift. This pattern also features the long single crochet. To do this insert the hook into the stitch, yarn over, and draw a loop through to have two loops on the hook. Yarn over again, draw through both loops on the hook. These are really just regular single stitches but worked in a row that isn't the regular working row.

You need white and green worsted weight wool and a size G Tunisian crochet hook.

Row 1: Use the white wool to chain 14, draw up a loop in the second chain from the hook. Draw up a loop in each remaining chain. Yarn over and draw through the one loop.

Row 2-12: Draw up a loop in each vertical bar to get 14 loops on your hook. Yarn over, draw through one loop.

Don't fasten off right now.

Now to work the border.

Row 1: Use the soft white to chain 1, sc evenly around the entire coaster base (use the pattern sc, chain 1, sc) in each corner stitch. Now you fasten off.

Row 2: Join the green yarn in any stitch you want. Sc in some of the places you placed the single stitches in row one, working the singles as you go. Sc in each sc, with three sc in each corner.

Fasten off and you're done.

One Skein Scarf

Scarves are nice but they can use up a lot of wool. Here's a pattern that uses only one skein of wool. This pattern uses the Tunisian double crochet. Just yarn over, slide the hook from right to left under the post of the stitch, draw up a loop, yarn over, and pull through two.

You need one skein of homespun yarn and a 9mm Afghan hook.

Start by chaining 15.

Row 1: With one loop on the needle, use a simple stitch across the chain and do your return row.

Row 2: Chain two (this counts as your first double crochet), then double crochet across the row. Then return as before.

Row 3: Repeat row one and two until the scarf is as long as you want it to be. When you're done bind off using sc.

Yes it really is that simple.

Knit headband

This headband is great for keeping you warm in the cold weather. It's pretty simple to make too. This pattern uses the special instruction "Make 1". You do this by inserting the hook knitwise through the fabric in the space between the stitches. Pull up the loop after.

This pattern works with any yarn and needle combination so find one that fits for you.

Get started by chaining 5.

Row 1: Pick up each loop across

Row2-5: Use a Tunisian knot stitch across the row

Row 6: find the centre stitch and knot stitch your way to it. Make 1, then knot stitch the centre stitch, make 1 again, then knot stitch your way across the rest of the row.

Rows 7-9: Knot stitch across the row.

Then just repeat row 6-9 until the scarf is 3.5 inches wide. Place a marker on the last increase row and measure the length from the beginning to that marker. Make a note of the measurement as "measurement A".

The total length of the headband should be about 18 inches. Remember that it's going to stretch when you put it on so it needs to be a few inches short. Double measurement A and subtract it from the size of the headband. This is measurement B and also needs to be noted. It'll be the main length of the headband. Continue in knot stitches across each row until you hit measurement B then it's time to start your decreases.

Row 1: find your centre stitch. Knot stitch across to one stitch before the center stitch. Skip that stitch and knot stitch the center stitch. Then skip the one after the center and knot stitch across the remaining stitches.

Row 2-4: Just knot stitch your way across the row

Repeat row 1-4 until only five stitches remain. Then complete one more row of knot stitches.

For the buttonhole row you need to find the center stitch again. Knot stitch across to the center stitch and skip it. Knot stitch from there to the end. On the return row you need to chain one for the skipped stitch.

Complete two more rows in knot stitches and bind off, and then fasten off to finish.

Ipod Hoodie

It's quite likely your kids have an iPod or iPhone. Because you use Tunisian stitches the hoodie is pretty thick and protective of whatever device they have.

You need sportweight cotton, and a size F needle.

To start with make a foundation of 14 chain stitches.

Row 1: Work your foundation row using simple stitch

Row 2: Work a row of knit stitches

Repeat row 2 until what you have is the size of your iPod and prepare to shape the collar.

The right side of the collar:

Row 1: Work a knot stitch in the first four stitches and finish as normal by leaving the rest of the row unworked. **Row 2** is an alternate to row 1 and what you do instead is work a knot stitch across while increasing between the last two stitches.

Row 3: Work a row of knot stitches

Row 4: Work knot stitches acrossing, increasing between the last two stitches

Row 5: Work a row of knot stitches

Repeat rows four and five until the number of loops is half of the number of chains you made in the first step.

Left side:

Join a separate piece of yarn into the unfinished row five stitches from the end. Work the same as you did on the right side but increase on the first two stitches, rather than the last two.

Then fasten off.

Pick up the stitch from the right side and work your way across the right side using knot stitches and across the left side.

Work in knot stitches until what you have fits up and over an iPod.

Hold the right sides together and then slip stitch the bottom, leaving an opening for the bottom port. Slip stitch up the sides.

Time to make the hood:

Chain an even number of stitches so that it fits around the opening. It should be around 18.

Work on even stitches using knot stitches for about eight rows and then decrease twice in the center of the next 2 or 3 rows.

Fold your work in half and whipstitch one side together for the top and then slip stitch the other end around the opening.

Lastly it's time to make the pocket:

Pick up a couple of stitches where you want your pocket to be and then work two rows of knot stitches. Then three rows decreasing at the beginning and end. Whipstitch the top down and you're done.

Kindle Cozy

Nothing like keeping a Kindle nice and warm between uses. Here's a handy little pattern to show you how.

You need two colors of worsted weight yarn and a MO-EZ hook. The gauge is that 6 rows should equal 2 inches.

You'll be using the Tunisian simple stitch for this. Start by chaining 18.

Row 1: Pick up a loop in every chain until the end (which is 18 loops) and do a basic return row on the way back.

Row 2-49: Pick up a loop in every vertical bar until the end (with 18 loops on the hook) and use a basic return row.

Row 50: Insert a hook through the next two vertical bars and pull up a loop. This is known as a decrease. Pull up a loop in each vertical bar until the last three stitches. Insert the hook into the next two bars and pull up a loop. Pull up a loop in the last stitch and use a basic return row.

Row 51: Repeat row 2.

Row 52: Repeat row 50

Row 53: Repeat row 2

Row 54: Repeat row 50.

Row 55 is the buttonhole row: Pull up a loop in each vertical bar for the first four stitches so you have five loops on the hook. Skip two bars and then pull up a loop in the remaining stitches, giving you ten loops on the hook. Return using a basic return except at the skipped stitches. With them you need to chain two and then complete the row.

Row 56: Pick up a loop in every vertical bar until the chain 2. Here you insert the hook into the space, making sure to go under the little bit of yarn made by skipping the stitch earlier. Pull up a loop and then keep pulling up a loop in the remaining bars. Use a basic return row.

Row 57: Repeat row 2

Row 58: This is the finish off row: Insert the hook into the vertical bar and pull up a loop. Pull the loop through the loop already on your hook, a slip stitch, and continue to the end of the row. If you're about to change color then finish off.

How to finish off: You need a kindle for this step. Or something the size of a kindle. Place the kindle on to the strip and then fold it over so you know where the sides meet. Hold the strip while removing the kindle to keep everything in place. Use a pin to help keep everything together. Take the second color and sc around the cozy, making sure you go through the thicknesses on both sides. It helps to start at the bottom of one side, go up and around the flap, and then down the other side. Now your kindle will always be nice and warm.

Knit stitch hat

We're finishing with another hat. This time it's a seamed hat that does wonders for keeping you warm.

You need two different colored sportsweight yarn, a J hook with the cable attached, and a tapestry needle.

Here's the pattern.

Chain 75 with your first color.

Row 1: With a loop on your hook, pick up each stitch across. Return your row like you normally would. Before you pull the hook through the last stitch you need to swap colors.

Row 2: Knit stitch across the row with a loop on your hook. Change the color on the last one of the return row again.

Row 3 onwards: Keep knitting across and repeating steps one and two, making sure to swap colors. Go until the piece is as long as you need it to be. Eight inches tall should give you a bit of a droop in your hat.

Decrease row 1: Knot stitch across each stitch. Yarn over on return row and pull through a loop. Yarn over and pull it through two more times. Yarn over and pull it through three. Yarn over and pull two three times, then yarn over and pull it through three. Repeat that step until you reach the end of the row.

Row 1A: Knot stich across with your second color, sliding the hook through the decreased stitches in the last return row. That ensures that they stay decreased ones.

Decrease row 2: Knot stitch each stitch across. On the return row, yarn over and pull through a loop. Yarn over and pull through two, yarn over and pull through three. Then yarn over and pull through 2 three times, and yarn over and pull through three. Then repeat that step until the end of the row once more.

Row 2A: Knit stitch across with another color, making the hook through the decreased stitches in the last return row. This will make sure they stay decreased, as before.

Decrease row 3: Knit stitch across like with the other decrease steps. On the return row, yarn over and pull through one loop. Yarn over and pull through two, yarn over and pull through three. Then yarn over and pull through 2 three times, and yarn over and pull through three. Then repeat that step until the end of the row once more.

Row 3A: Knit stitch across with another color, making the hook through the decreased stitches in the last return row. This will make sure they stay decreased, as before.

Decrease row 4: Knit stitch each stitch across. On the return row yarn over and pull through three. Repeat the yarn over step until the end of the row.

Row 4a: Knit stitch across with another color, making the hook through the decreased stitches in the last return row. This will make sure they stay decreased, as before. There's no need to change color this time though. You should have fifteen stitches by this point. Cut the yarn, leaving a long tail of the last color used.

Time to finish up!

Thread the yarn through the tapestry needle and insert the needle on the left of the piece. It needs to go through the last row. Slide the needle through every stitch and pull the work snugly. The top of the hat must be gathered.

Turn the work over with the right sides and use the mattress stitch seaming it all together. After that you can get rid of the curling by blocking it or adding a brim. Or you can just accept it. Either way your hat is now complete.

Squares, Stripes, and Solids

Textured Tunisian Afghan

This unique blanket uses a combination of the Tss stitch and a triple crochet stitch for the cables. This blanket is done in a solid color; the image shows the blanket done in white but you can choose any color you like.

Tunisian Cable Blanket

(Tunisian Cable Blanket, 2015)

Skill Level: Beginner-Intermediate

- Materials needed: 6 skeins of sport weight yarn any color. The blanket uses two strands held together as one.

- Any size afghan hook, the size determines the size of the stitch and that is up to you with this pattern

- Yarn needle

Finished Size: You can make this blanket any length you want. Just finish and tie off when you are happy with the length.

Pattern

Tc panel and make 3

Row 1: Ch 27

Row 2: Make two rows of Tss

Row 3 Part A: Tss in the 1st three sts. In the 4th st make tc as follows-Yo twice, insert hook in vertical bar two rows below, Yo and pull through 2 loops, Yo and pull through 2 loops, leave 1 loop on the hook. Tss st in next 3 sts, tc in 4th st, repeat across then end with 3 tss.

Row 3 Part B: Tss as 2nd pass

Row 4 Part A: Tss in 1st three sts. In 4th st, make tc st as follows-Yo twice, insert hook in vertical bar two rows below, Yo and pull through 2 loops, Yo and pull through 2 loops and leave 1 look on the hook. Tss in next 3 sts, tc in 4th st, across and end with 3 tc sts.

Row 4 Part B: Tss at 2nd pass

Repeat rows 4A and 4B until desired length is reached and bind off with tss

Make 2 Tss panels as long as the others.

Finishing

Join panels with the wrong sides facing, alternated between the cabled sections and the plain panels. Attach the panels from behind using the loops on the backside of the work.

Minty Squares Tunisian Blanket

This pattern resembles traditional crochet granny squares but the stitch used is the Tunisian Simple Stitch. The colors used for this pattern are listed in the directions but feel free to substitute any colors you like. The pattern uses traditional crochet abbreviations.

- Materials needed: Red Heart "super-saver" yarn. A) 3 skeins of soft-white, 1 skein each of, B) cornmeal, C) country blue, D) pale plum, E) frosty green and F) light raspberry

- 6.5 Afghan hook

- 6mm crochet hook

- Yarn needle

Finished size: 43" X 60.5"

Pattern

This blanket is created from blocks, similar to the way a granny blanket is created. For this pattern you will need 7 blocks of each color yarn. To begin, use the 6mm crochet hook and ch 16.

Make 2 tss panels the same length as the other panels

Row 1: Keep all loops on the hook. Pull a loop through the second ch in the hook and through each of the ch until you have 16 loops on the hook. Without turning, work back, Yo and pull through 1 loop, Yo and pull through 2 loops, continue until you have removed 15 loops and one loop is left on the hook

Row 2: With the yarn at the back of the work, draw up a loop through the next vertical bar/stitch, *with the yarn in the front of the work, draw up a loop through the next vertical bar*7 times. With the yarn at the back of the work, draw a loop through the last loop, there is now 16 loops on the hook. Work back without turning, *Yo and draw through 1 loop, Yo and draw through 2 loops*15 times.

Row 3: With the yarn at the front of the work, draw up a loop through the next vertical bar/stitch, "with the yarn in back of the work, draw up a loop through the next vertical bar*7 times. With the yarn at the front of the work, draw up a loop through the last loop, there is now 16 loops on the hook. Without turning, Yo and pull through 1 loop, Yo and pull through 2 loops, continue until you have removed 15 loops and one loop is left on the hook.

Row 4-13: Repeat rows 2-3 5 times

Row 14: *With the yarn at the back of the work, draw a loop through the next vertical bar and through the loop on the hook. With the yarn at the front of the work, draw a loop through the next vertical bar and through the loop on the hook* 7 times. With the yarn at the back of the work, draw a loop through the next vertical bar and through the loop on the hook and tie off

One block is now complete. Repeat steps 1 through 14 7 times in each color yarn.

Block Boarders

Round 1: With the right side facing the front, use the 6mm crochet hook and Join color A in the top right hand corner stitch and ch 3. *Skip the next stitch, dc, ch1 dc in the next stitch 6 times. Skip next stitch, dc in last stitch, ch2 and turn to work down the side, dc in first row end, dc, ch1, dc, in the next row end, skip next row end, dc, ch1, dc 5 times skip next row end, dc in next row end, ch 2* Turn and work across lower edge, dc in 1st stitch, repeat *to* one more time, now join with a slip stitch in top of ch 3 then tie off.

Round 2: With the same color as center block, join st in same st as joining, ch1, sc in same stitch. *ch1, sc in next ch – 1 space 6 times. Ch1 skip next dc, sc in next dc, now sc, ch2, sc in the corner ch, 2nd stitch, sc in next dc, ch1, sc in next ch – 1 space 6 times. Ch1, skip next dc, sc in next dc, sc, ch2, sc in the corner ch 2nd stitch*. Sc in next dc, now repeat *to* one more time, now join in first sc and tie off.

Round 3: Join A in top right hand corner, ch-2nd stitch, ch3, dc, ch2, dc2, all in the same stitch. *skip next sc. Dc in next sc, 2dc in next stitch 7 times. Skip next sc, dc in next sc. 2dc, ch2, 2dc, in the 2nd corner stitch. Repeat from * **around the block, now join in top of ch3 and tie off.**

Assemble the Blanket

B	D	E	F	C
F	C	B	D	E
D	E	F	C	B
C	B	D	E	F
E	F	C	B	D
B	D	E	F	C
F	C	B	D	E

ASSEMBLY DIAGRAM

Arrange the blocks according to the diagram, using the 6mm crochet hook, join the blocks together from the back, through the back loops using a slip stitch.

Peppermint Twist Afghan

This afghan is simple to do and looks great anytime of year. This pattern is worked with two strands of yarn held together and crocheted as one. The simple afghan stitch and the double yarn makes this a cozy blanket for cold winter nights.

- Materials needed: Red Heart supersaver or classic or any brand 4-ply worsted. 35oz of cherry red, 28oz of white, and 12oz of paddy green

- 10in size P double ended crochet hook

- Size N traditional crochet hook

  Yarn needle

Finished Size: 51" x 67"

Pattern

Row 1: Using the double crochet hook, ch 23 holding 2 strands of cherry red as one. Insert into 2nd ch from hook and Yo and pull through adding a loop to the hook. *insert hook into next ch, Yo and pull through adding another loop to the hook* until there are 23 loops on the hook. Slide all of the stitches to the other side of the hook, turn the hook so the loops are on the left side. Leave the cherry red yarn uncut, it will be used later.

Row 2: Hold and use two strands of white yarn as one. Using the white strands, make a slip knot on the left side of the hook and pull the white through the loop on the hook. *Work from left to right and Yo, pull through 2 loops on the hook, one of each color (remember two strands together is one loop)* until there is only one loop left on the hook.

Row 3: Do not turn the work. Work from right to left with the white yarn. Insert the hook into the 2nd stitch from the hook, pull through, leave the loop on the hook, insert the hook through the next vertical bar, Yo and pull through a new loop. *Skip the next vertical bar and insert hook into the next horizontal stitch, Yo and pull through, insert hook under next vertical stitch, Yo and pull through leaving the loop on the hook* Repeat * to* until there are 23 loops on the hook. Slide stitches to other side of hook and leave the yarn uncut.

Row 4: Turn hook and use both strands of cherry red yarn as one. Work from left to right, Yo and pull yarn through first loop on the hook. *Yo and pull through next loop on the hook, now there are 2 loops on the hook* Repeat * to * until 1 loop remains on the hook.

Row 5: Repeat row 3 with cherry red

Row 6: Repeat row 4 with white

Rows 7-144 Repeat rows 3 through 6 then end with a Row 4

Row 145: Work from right to left with cherry red, ch 1 and skip the first vertical bar. * Insert the hook into the top of the next horizontal stitch, Yo and pull through the stitch and the loop on the hook* Repeat * to * until end of row. Tie off the cherry red and cut the white.

Edging

Join two strands of paddy green held together as one to any dc corner with sc.

work 3 scs in each corner dc, (dc in skipped st or row, below next ch – 1 sp, sc in next dc) to next corner repeat * to * around, end last repeat with slip stitch in beginning sc, tie off.

Add edging to two more strips in the same way, then turn the remaining strips over so the white side is facing and add edging the same way.

Assembly

Face one red side to one white side and whip stitch with the yarn needle through the back loops only using paddy green.

Outer Afghan Edging

Join paddy green using a slip stitch, then use a hdc in each stitch around, finish and join with a slip stitch and tie off.

Finish off the afghan by weaving in any loose yarn with the yarn needle.

Baby Blankets and Throws

Baby blankets and throws are smaller than the average afghan or blanket. For beginners it may be easier to crochet a baby blanket or throw because the patterns are shorter and it takes less time to complete.

Most patterns for Tunisian baby blankets and throws use the Tunisian simple stitch and not much else. Although these baby blankets and throws use the Tunisian simple stitch, some also use other techniques for decoration or to add interest to the finished project.

All the patterns in this book are perfect for beginners and intermediate crocheters but that does not mean they are simple looking or boring. The Tunisian stitch itself adds a special character to ordinary blankets that traditional crochet stitches like the single or double crochet do not have.

These patterns are perfect for warming up family member in the living room or cuddling a new baby with warmth and a touch of love. Although some of the patterns have instructions for color, feel free to choose any colors you wish and switch them out with the ones listed. The important part is to make sure you buy the right amount of yarn for each project.

There are differences in yarn, they differ in thickness or strand amount and the thread used for creating the yarn. Some yarns use only natural dyes and natural fibers and yarns like baby yarn is softer and a bit thinner than a wool or wool blend yarn. Choose a yarn that is compatible with the project you are creating and be sure to buy the right number of skeins to finish the project.

Entrelac Baby Blanket

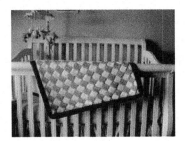

This Entrelac baby blanket has a diamond pattern and solid border. The pattern uses standard abbreviations and the Tunisian simple stitch. The design is in the pattern not the stitch. Learn to crochet with an Entrelac style will add a new skill to your crochet repertoire and you can apply it in your own creations when you begin making your own blankets.

Entrelac may seem daunting for those who are beginners but looks can be deceiving. Unlike some crochet items that use special stitches and techniques to create a beautiful blanket, Entrelac uses only one stitch. Using multiple colors for an Entrelac blanket can resemble a quilt. Using only one color for Entrelac blankets will still give it a distinct look. The alternating squares/diamonds create a textured pattern that is distinct from row to row.

Once you learn the technique of Entrelac you can use it to create anything you want. This style looks great for hats, socks, scarves, pillows…the list goes on.

The Entrelac technique never fails to impress and the finished project looks like you spent forever on it. This is one technique that has been borrowed from knitting that works really well for Tunisian crochet.

Entrelac Baby Blanket Pattern

Skill Level: Beginner-intermediate

- Materials Needed: Two contrasting colors of medium weight yarn, one color for A and one color for B. 500 yards of each color.

- Size 10 Tunisian crochet hook/Afghan hook

- Yarn needle

Pattern

Notes about this pattern

- The return pass is created: *Yo pull through two loops and repeat from * across

- Binding off: Insert the hook from the front to the back between two vertical bars of the stitch then Yo and pull up a loop, then Yo and pull through both loops on the hook

- Picking up loops from the bind off row: Insert the hook through two loops of the bind off chain then Yo and pull up a loop

- M1 means Make one stitch: Insert the hook from the front between the next two vertical bars then Yo and pull up a loop

- Pay attention to the tension you are using, try to keep an even tension while you work, not too tight, not too loose

-

Begin with Color A and Ch 74

The first tier will have twelve base triangles

Row 1: Insert hook in second St from the hook, Yo and pull up a loop, now there are 2 loops on the hook then return pass

Row 2: M1 then Tks in the next vertical bar. Now insert the hook in the next ch and pull up a loop. There should be 4 loops on the hook, now return pass

Row 3: Tks in the next two vertical bars then M1 between the last vertical bar and the edge of the last row. Insert the hook in the next ch and pull up a loop, now there are 5 loops on the hook, then return pass

Row 4: Tks in the next 3 vertical bars, M1 between the last vertical bar and the edge of the last row. Insert the hook in the next ch and pull up a loop, now there are 6 loops on the hook, then return pass

Row 5: Tks in the next 4 vertical bars, M1 between the last vertical bar and the edge of the last row. Insert the hook in the next ch and pull up a loop, now there are 7 loops on the hook, then return pass

Row 6: Tks in the next 5 vertical bars, M1 between the last vertical bar and the edge of the last row. Insert the hook in the next ch and pull up a loop, now there are 8 loops on the hook, then return pass

Row 7: Bind off 6 stitches. Slst in same ch as the last stitch in the last row. One triangle is now complete

Repeat rows 1-7 11 more times so there are 12 triangles, on the last triangle Slst in the last ch and tie off

Tier A is 1 left triangle, 11 squares, and 1 right triangle

Right-Edge Triangle

Join color B in the bottom corner of the first triangle made or in the last edge of the previous right-edge triangle for successive tiers

Row 1: Ch 2 then pull up a loop in the second ch from the hook in the edge of the last row of the first tier. Now there are 3 loops on the hook, then return pass

Row 2: M1 then Tks in the next vertical bar in the edge of the 2nd row of the first tier, now there are 4 loops on the hook, then return pass

Row 3: M1 then Tks in the next 2 vertical bars and in the edge of the 3rd row of the last tier, now there are 5 loops on the hook, then return pass

Row 4: M1 then Tks in the next 3 vertical bars and in the edge of the 4th row of the last tier, now there are 6 loops on the hook, then return pass

Row 5: M1 then Tks in the next 4 vertical bars and in the edge of the 5th row of the last tier, now there are 7 loops on the hook, then return pass

Row 6: M1 then Tks in the next 5 vertical bars and in the edge of the 6th row of the last tier, now there are 8 loops on the hook, then return pass

Row 7: Bind off 6 stitches then Slst in the next stitch of the last tier

Square

Row 1: Pick up 7 stitches from the edge of the last tier, now there are 8 loops on the hook, then return pass

Rows 2-6: Tks in the next 6 vertical bars and in the edge of the next row of the last tier, now there are 8 loops on the hook, then return pass

Row 7: Bind off 6 stitches then Slst in the next stitch of the last tier

Repeat 1-7 10 more times so there are 11 squares made

Left-Edge Triangle

Row 1: Pick up 7 stitches from the edge of the last tier, now there are 8 loops on the hook, then return pass

Row 2: Tks across, now there are 7 loops on the hook, then return pass

Row 3: Tks across, now there are 6 loops on the hook, then return pass

Row 4: Tks across, now there are 5 loops on the hook, then return pass

Row 5: Tks across, now there are 4 loops on the hook, then return pass

Row 6: Tks across, now there are 3 loops on the hook, then return pass

Row 7: Bind off 1 stitch then tie off the yarn

Tier B has 12 squares

Join color A in the first stitch of the last tier and work 12 squares the same as you did for Tier A

Now repeat tier A and then tier B 8 times, now repeat tier A one last time

Finishing Tier has 12 triangles

Join color A to the first stitch of the last tier

Row 1: Pick up 7 stitches from the edge of the last tier, now there are 8 loops on the hook, then return pass

Row 2: Skip the next vertical bar and Tks in the next 5 vertical bars and in the edge of the next row of the last tier, now there are 7 loops on the hook, then return pass

Row 3: Skip the next vertical bar and Tks in the next 4 vertical bars and in the edge of the next row of the last tier, now there are 6 loops on the hook, then return pass

Row 4: Skip the next vertical bar and Tks in the next 3 vertical bars and in the edge of the next row of the last tier, now there are 5 loops on the hook, then return pass

Row 5: Skip the next vertical bar and Tks in the next 2 vertical bars and in the edge of the next row of the last tier, now there are 4 loops on the hook, then return pass

Row 6: Skip the next vertical bar and Tks in the next vertical bar and in the edge of the next row of the last tier, now there are 3 loops on the hook, then return pass

Row 7: Skip the next vertical bar and Slst in the next stitch of the last tier, one triangle is now complete

Repeat rows 1-7 11 more times until there are 12 triangles then fasten off the end

Block the blanket

Weave in all loose ends

Striped Afghan Throw

This pretty afghan can be used as a throw or baby blanket. To make it a throw blanket use a heavier yarn, for a baby blanket use baby yarn for a super soft touch. Use any colors you like for the stripes just follow the instructions for how much you need of each color to complete the throw.

- Materials needed: Patons SWS, 110 yards of each color: A) Natural Earth

  B) Natural Russet and C) Natural Charcoal.

- Size L traditional crochet hook

- Size N Afghan hook

- Yarn needle

Finished Size: 36" x 56"

Pattern

As you finish each row, you will have the previous strand of color waiting, pick up the new color and continue.

This pattern uses the Tss exclusively, for a refresher on the Tss stitch review the stitches in chapter 1.

Color Sequence/Pattern

1: Ch 108 with color A

2: Forward pass, continue with color A

3: Return pass, drop color A and add color B

4: Forward pass, drop color B and add color C

Repeat 2-4 until you have reached your desired length or 56"

Create the finishing row using slip stitches using the traditional crochet hook

Tunisian Lap Blanket

- Materials needed: Two colors of yarn, yarn A) 2 skeins, each 104 yards

  Yarn B) 2 skeins, each 104 yards

- Afghan hook size 1

- Yarn needle

Finished Size: 26" x 14"

Pattern

Ch 62 for beginning row

Using only the Tunisian simple stitch/Tss, work 78 rows. Alternate between color A and color B. Use color A on the forward passes and use color B on the return pass. After each pass, leave one color and pick up the next color, do not cut the yarn, leave it until you return to pick it up.

After the last return row, bind off with slip stitches.

Tunisian Afghan in the Round

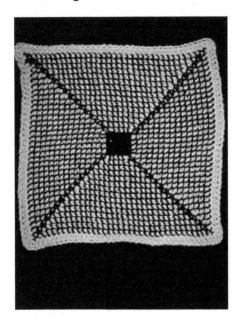

- Materials needed: Worsted weight yarn in two colors, one for color A and one for color B. Three skeins of each color.

- Size 10.5 double ended Tunisian crochet hook

- Yarn needle

Finished Size: As large or small as you like, continue or end when you decide it is large enough.

Pattern

Color A will always be worked with the right side facing you and color B will always be worked with the wrong side facing you.

Corner Increase is done as follows: Tss into the stitch, Yo and Tss into the stitch again, this creates 3 stitches in 1.

Using color A, ch 4

Round 1: In 4th ch from hook, 2 dc, ch 1, *3 dc, ch 1* repeat * to * 2 times. Join with a slst in top of ch 3. 12 dc, 4 ch in 1 space.

Round 2: Keep the first loop on the hook. *Insert hook into next dc, Yo and pull through* repeat * to * one time. Insert hook into ch 1 space, Yo and pull through. Yo and insert into ch 1 space again, Yo and pull through, now there are 6 loops on the hook.

Turn the work and push the work to other side of hook. Using color B return pass on the back side of the work by Yo and pull through 1st loop, then Yo and pull through 2 loops and repeat until 2 loops remain on the hook.

*Turn and push work to the other side. Using color A, pick up the loops in each dc. Insert hook in ch 1 space, Yo and pull through, now Yo and insert hook in ch 1 space again, Yo and pull through.

Turn work and push to other side. Using color B, return pass by Yo and pull through 2 loops on the hook, repeat until 2 loops remain on the hook.*

Repeat from * to * 2 more times. Do not join at end of round. 24 stitches

Chapter 3 – Simple Patterns

Tunisian Scarf

For this scarf, you will need 7 skeins of yarn any color, and a J gauge Afghan hook. The completed scarf is 12in wide and 72in long.

Ch 42 then insert the hook into the second stitch from the hook, Yo and pull through the stitch and leave the loop on the hook, continue until the end of the row. This is the foundation row and the preparation row.

Now begin the first return row. Insert the hook into the second stitch from the hook, Yo and pull through the loop. *Insert the hook into the next two stitches, Yo and pull through both. Repeat * until the end of the row.

Now begin the forward row. Insert the hook through the first vertical stitch, Yo and pull through, continue until the forward row is complete. Continue making return and forward rows until the fabric is 70in. long. Now finish off, cut the yarn and weave the end into the last row.

Alternate Pattern for a Striped Scarf and a Color Block Scarf

To make this scarf using two colors or more choose and purchase complimenting colors of yarn. Make sure to purchase 7 skeins all together. To make stripes, change colors every two returns. To make color block, change colors every twelve returns.

Striped Pot Holders

You will need two contrasting colors of yarn, one skein of each color. A J Gauge Afghan hook, and a yarn needle. The finished pot holder will be 8in x 8in with a loop for hanging.

Ch 42 then using the same color insert the hook into the second stitch from the hook, Yo and pull the yarn through the stitch, leave the loop on the hook. This is the foundation and preparation row.

Start the first return row with the second color, *complete two rows, one return and one forward, then change colors. Rep * until 8 rows are completed and finish off. Weave the end into the last row using a yarn needle.

To make the loop for hanging, insert the hook into the corner of the fabric and Ch 10. Now insert the hook into the same corner, Yo and pull through. Cut the yarn and weave the end into the last row with a yarn needle.

Thick and Thirsty Wash Cloth

You will need one skein of 100% cotton yarn. The finished wash cloth will be an 8in x 8in square. Follow the instructions on the skein for fabric care. Work the stitches loosely so the fabric will not curl up.

To begin, Ch 42 do not turn the work, Yo and pull through the second stitch from the hook. Leave the loop on the hook, *Yo and pull through each stitch and leave each loop on the hook, Rep * until the end of the row, there is now 42 loops on the hook. This is the preparation and foundation row.

Without turning the project, Yo and pull through the second loop on the hook, *Yo and pull through the next two loops on the hook. Rep * until the end of the row. Without turning the work, pick up the first vertical stitch and begin the forward row. Continue making return and forward rows until the fabric has 8 rows then finish off.

Alternate Patterns for Striped Wash Cloth and a Boarder Wash Cloth

To make a striped wash cloth, purchase two complimenting colors of cotton yarn, one skein each. Change colors every two return rows. To add a border to a solid color wash cloth, use a contrasting color of yarn and insert the hook into a corner of the wash cloth. Ch 1, and insert the hook into the first chain, Yo and pull through, insert the hook into the same stitch, Yo and pull through, do this four times on each corner. Then insert the hook into the second stitch from the hook, *Yo and pull the yarn through the loop. Continue to Rep * until the border surrounds the wash cloth.

Two Tone Throw Pillow

This pattern requires two contrasting colors of yarn, one skein of each color. One bag of polyester fill, a J gauge Afghan hook, and a yarn needle. The finished pillow is approximately 12in x 12in. One 12in square will be one color and the other 12in square will be a contrasting color.

Ch 42, then insert the hook into the second stitch from the hook, *Yo and pull through, leave the loop on the hook. Rep * until the row is complete. This is the foundation and preparation rows.

Begin the return row, Ch 1, *Yo and pull through two stitches/loops on the hook. Rep * until only one loop remains on the hook. Begin the forward row, *insert the hook into the next vertical stitch, Yo and pull through, leave a loop on the hook. Rep * until the row is complete then finish off.

Alternate between the return row and the forward row until 12 rows have been completed. Using the contrasting color follow the same instructions and create a 12 in square. Using the yarn needle, sew both squares together leaving a small gap so the pillow can be stuffed. Stuff the pillow then stitch gap closed and the pillow is complete.

7 - Striped Granny Square

The granny square is a great way to use up left over yarn. One skein will make several granny squares. The squares can be used to create scarves, throws, and pillows, just sew the squares together using a yarn needle. This granny square is striped and when complete it is 12in x 12in. Use a J gauge Afghan hook.

Ch 42, then insert the hook into the second stitch from the hook. *Yo and pull through stitch and leave the loop on the hook. Rep * until the row is complete and one loop remains on the hook. This is the foundation and preparation rows.

Change colors and begin the return row, Ch 1, * Yo and pull through the next two loops on the hook, Rep * until the end of the row, leave one loop on the hook. Now begin the forward row, * insert the hook into the next vertical stitch, Yo and pull through leaving a loop on the hook. Rep * until the row is complete.

Continue changing colors every two rows until 12 rows are completed. Finish off and weave the end into the fabric. To create a boarder around the granny square, choose a color and * Ch 1 in any corner of the fabric. In the same stitch, insert the hook and Ch 1 three more times. Now there are four stitches in the corner of the fabric. ** Insert the hook into the next stitch, Yo and pull through both stitches leaving one loop on the hook. Rep ** until the row reaches the next corner, now Rep * and begin the next section. Rep ** until the next corner then Rep*. Continue this until the entire square has a boarder. Finish off and weave the loose end into the fabric with a yarn needle.

8 – Crazy Granny Square Throw

Using pattern 7, the striped granny square, create 15 squares. Each square is 12in x 12in so the finished throw will be 3ft wide and 5ft long. Lay out the granny squares in a pattern. Place one square with the stripes in a horizontal position, the next square with the stripes in a vertical position, and the third square with the stripes in a horizontal position then sew the squares end to end using a yarn needle. Every grouping is three squares across. For the next row, place the first square with the stripes in a vertical position, the next in a horizontal position, and the last one in a vertical position, then sew them end to end using a yarn needle. Alternate between both patterns until all five rows are complete.

Now sew each row to the next until all five rows are sew together one on top of the other. To give the throw a finished look, choose one of the colors in the stripes and begin in a corner. Place four crochet stitches in each corner as the boarder progresses. Crochet using a single crochet stitch around the entire throw.

9 - Warm and Comfy Cowl

To complete this cowl you will need two skeins of yarn any color and a J gauge Afghan hook. This cowl is approximately 15in long. Begin the project with Ch 50, insert the hook into the second stitch from the hook, Yo and pull through leaving one loop on the hook. Continue this until the row is complete. These are the preparation and foundation rows.

To begin the return row, Ch 1 then Yo and pull through the loop. * Yo and pull through two loops on the hook. Rep * until the return row is complete and one loop remains on the hook.

To begin the forward row, * insert the hook into the next vertical stitch, Yo and pull through leaving one loop on the hook. Rep * until the end of the row.

Alternate between the return and forward row until there are 15 rows completed, then finish off the last row. To make sure the fabric lays properly and does not curl, it should be blocked. To block the fabric and remove any curling, use push pins and pin the fabric down on a thick piece of cardboard or cork board. Stretch the fabric where it needs it to create a perfect rectangle. Spray the fabric lightly with warm water and leave it to air dry. When the pins are removed, the fabric will lay flat.

To finish the cowl, sew both ends of the rectangle together using a yarn needle. The finished project is thick, cozy, cowl that defies the worst winter has to offer. This pattern can be altered to size, just change the original number of Ch stitches in the beginning to reflect the width and the number of rows to reflect the length.

10 -Simple Cozy Wrist Warmers

Wrist warmers are a fun and fashionable way to keep warm while texting. Wrist warmers cover the palms, wrists, and part of the arm but the fingers and thumb are exposed. This pattern requires two skeins of yarn, a J gauge Afghan hook, and a yarn needle. The finished wrist warmers will be 12 in long.

Ch 42 then insert the hook into the second stitch from the hook. Yo and pull through the stitch leaving one loop on the hook. * Insert the hook into the next stitch, Yo and pull through leaving one stitch on the hook. Rep * until the row is complete. These are the foundation and preparation rows.

Ch 1 then Yo and pull the yarn through the stitch, * Yo and pull through the next two stitches. Rep * until the return row is complete and one loop is left on the hook.

*Insert the hook into the next vertical stitch, Yo and pull through leaving a loop on the hook. Rep * until the forward row is complete and one loop is left on the hook.

Alternate between the return and forward rows until the fabric has 12 rows. The fabric is now 12 in long, you can change the width of the wrist warmers for size by adding or deleting rows until the fabric wraps around the wrist and fits snug but not tight.

Finish the warmers by folding the fabric in half and sewing the seam long ways. As the sewing gets closer to the top of the warmer, leave a 2in gap for the thumb. The warmers are now complete but decorative stitching or any other embellishment may be added to personalize the warmers.

Create Your Own Pattern

Once you have learned the simple Tunisian stitch, you can use your new skill to create your own patterns. To create your own pattern you will need count the number of chain stitches you will use, and count the number of rows your project will need.

Begin the pattern with information about the amount of yarn needed, the hook used, any other tools needed and the size of the project. The next step is use the abbreviations to explain how to work your pattern.

Before you create any pattern try it out first to be sure it is what you want it to be. Any pattern you create can be shared with others or just created for yourself. With a little practice and patience you will be able to create patterns and project yourself.

Chapter 4 – Easy Patterns for Projects

When you are working with these patterns, you are going to see that there is a pattern to the patterns. Most crochet projects are made up of the same basic form, and you are going to notice that you'll get better at the stitches themselves.

When you do these patterns, focus on keeping your stitches even and neat. You don't want there to be any loose ends, or any holes in your projects! This is something that is going to take patience to learn, but you are going to get it when you are persistent.

Take your time with these patterns, and make sure you are keeping your tension even and consistent. You may need to pull out some ends and put them back in again to get the right consistency, but you will get it. It just takes time and effort, but if you are going to get good at this craft, those are two qualities that you are going to want to have.

We used acrylic yarn for these patterns, but wool is always a good option for any blanket that you will use in the winter. Use baby soft yarn for the baby blanket, and make super soft for that little bundle of joy in your life!

You are more than welcome to use whatever yarn you like for any of these projects. That is part of what makes this hobby so unique for anyone!

All Season Afghan

6 balls of acrylic yarn in the color of your choice.

Cast on 400. Tunisian crochet all the way back across, you may need to use a holder to get all of the stitches to stay on. When you have reached the other side, chain 2, then double crochet all the way back to the first end.

Now, chain 2, then double crochet in the first stitch, chain 1, skip 1, chain 2, and double crochet in the next stitch. Repeat this pattern all the way across the row. Chain 2, turn, and double crochet in every stitch back across to the beginning.

Chain 2, turn, and double crochet in every other stitch across the row. Keep doing this until you have reached a square length with your afghan. Tie off, then crochet a border around the edge.

Patchwork Quilts

Scrap yarn works great for these, otherwise use 6 balls of various colors.

Cast on 15, then single crochet a square that is 15 stitches wide by the same height. Do this 8 times. Repeat this pattern, only this time do it with double crochet, for 8 squares.

Once you have all of your pieces, you can either crochet or sew them together into a nice patchwork quilt.

Long and Lean Snuggle Buddies

Cast on 20. Double crochet across the row, chain 2, turn, and double crochet back across. Repeat this step until you have a panel that is 6 feet long. Tie off. Make a second panel the same way, then sew the two together.

Stuff with a lot of stuffing, if you like firmer pillows. Otherwise, let them be a little under-stuffed for a lighter, squishier cuddle buddy.

Chapter 5 – Following a Pattern to the Letter

If you are at all familiar with crochet, you know that patterns tend to have some variations in them to make them fit you and your needs. For some patterns, however, it is important that you follow them to the letter, or you may not get the results that you want.

When you are working these patterns, make sure you follow each and every step, and that you pull out your work and do it again. This is an aspect that can be frustrating, but it is necessary if you want to get good at this style. While this is all about long and drapey projects, you still need it to be even.

What better way to learn how to do this project than to practice? This is the point of this chapter, and you need to make sure that you are following patterns. Practice as much as you can with these, and apply what you learn when you follow other patterns that may not have the same level of fluctuation that other patterns have.

We used acrylic yarn for these projects, but you can use whatever you like for them, make sure you use bright and cheery colors as much as you can!

Place Mats

Use a bamboo yarn.

Chain 15, then single crochet in each stitch. Chain 1, turn, and single crochet in each stitch across this once again. Repeat this step 25 times. Tie off, then add a fringe border to each placemat.

Crochet Beanie

Another common crocheted item is hats. This is one of the many kinds of hats you can make with Tunisian crochet.

You need one skein of soft wool, a size I Afghan hook, and a yarn needle. The gauge is that nineteen rows of nineteen stitches should give you a 5 inch square.

Row 1: Your foundation row needs to be a chain stitch of 36. Skip the first chain and pull up loops in the back bump of the other chains. Close by yarning over and pull through one loop on the hook. Yarn over and pull through two loops on the hook until you reach the end.

Row 2: Skip the first vertical bar. Working with a Tunisian full stitch insert your hook under the next 23 horizontal bars. Pull up a loop in each, giving you 24 loops on the hook. Close it by following the previous closing steps.

Row 3: Skip first vertical bar and first horizontal bar. Use a Tunisian full stitch and insert your hook under the next 23 horizontal bars, pulling up loops in each. Follow the same closing instructions.

Beauty Blankets

2 skeins acrylic yarn, and 2 balls fun fir yarn.

Cast on 45, then double crochet in each stitch across. Chain 2 at the end of the row, then double crochet in the next stich, chain 1, skip 1, then double crochet in the next stitch, all the way across.

Once you are happy with the size of your blanket, tie off. Crochet a border of fun fir around the edge of your blanket.

Envelope Pillow

1 skein acrylic yarn, 1 large button.

Cast on 25, then single crochet across. Chain 1, turn, and single crochet back across. Repeat this step until you have a perfect square. Tie off and make a second. Once you have reached the top of your second pillow, decrease your row by 1 stitch on each side.

Repeat this decrease until you are 10 rows up.

Next, sew the squares together, leaving the flap out. Stuff the pillows, then fold the flap over. Sew the button on as a final touch to make it have that envelope look.

Flirty Skirt

Measure your waist, add 2 inches, then cast on the length of this figure. Single crochet all the way across the row, chain 2, then double crochet back.

Chain 3, then double crochet in the 3rd chain from the hook. Repeat this on the other side. Continue to increase each row and double crochet in every stitch until you are at a length of 18 inches.

Tie off, and sew up the loos side. Crochet another chain, then feed that through the top of this skirt. When you are wearing it, this is your drawstring.

Cutie Pie Clutch

Scrap yarn works well for this, or you can use 1 ball fancy yarn.

Cast on 15, then double crochet in each stitch across. Work this pattern until you are 5 inches tall. Tie off and repeat on the other side, only make that one 8 inches tall. Sew them together as you did with the pillow in the last pattern, leaving the flap open.

Attach a button, and add a string as a button loop to the flap. Tie off and make sure everything is secure, and that's it!

Chapter 6 – Making an Unusual Pattern

The Delicious Table Runner

Use a light and delicate yarn for this.

Measure the width of your table, then cast on a length that is equal to 1 third this amount. Single crochet the first row, chain 8, skip 3, and single crochet in the next row.

Repeat this all the way across the row. To start row 2, chain 1, single crochet in the first stitch that is closest to the hook, then chain 8. Skip the next stich, then slip stitch into the loop you created in row 1.

Chain 8, then slip stitch into the next row. Repeat this pattern across to the other side, then repeat the beginning of row 2 again. Continue to work your runner, until you are happy with the length. Finish with another row of single crochet, and tie off.

Tunisian Crochet bookmark

This is a handy little bookmark for both kids and adults to enjoy their favorite books with.

You will only need a small amount of yarn. You'll also need a size G hook. You also don't need to worry about a gauge.

The foundation chain needs to be ten chain stitches long.**Row 1**: Insert the hook into the second chain from the hook. Yarn over and draw up a loop. Insert the hook into the next chain, yarn over, and draw up a loop. Repeat until done.

Row 2: Insert hook under the second vertical bar of the previous row. Yarn over and draw up a loop. Insert the hook under the next vertical bar, yarn over, and draw up a loop. Repeat until done.

Row 3-38: Repeat row 2. At the end of row 38, with just one loop left, fasten off and sew in the end. You have a small little rectangle that makes an ideal bookmark.

Tunisian dishcloth

This is more one for kids to make than one made for kids, but here's a simple little pattern for a colorful dishcloth

You need 1 ball of white worsted weight cotton, 1 ball of pink worsted weight cotton, a size G Tunisian crochet hook, and a yarn needle.

Row 1: Use the white cotton to chain 25. Bring up a loop in each chain across. Yarn over and pull two loops up on the hook. Repeat that until back at the start.

Row 2: Insert the hook in the hump just above the next vertical bar. Bring up a loop. Insert the hook into the next vertical bar. Bring up a loop. Repeat that across and then finish as you did before.

Row 3-17: Repeat row 2. Then fasten off the white cotton.

Now to work on the perimeter.

Round 1: Join the pink cotton in the top right corner on row 17 sc. Chain 2 sc in that corner. Sc in each stitch going across, sc, chain 2, sc in the corner. Sc in each row down the left side. Sc, chain 2 in the next corner. Sc in each stitch across the bottom. Sc, chain 2, sc in the next corner. Sc in each row up the right side. Join it together using a slip stitch in the first sc you made.

Round 2: Slip stitch into the first chain 2 sc, chain three, dc, chain 2, 2dc in the same sp. Dc in each sc across. 2dc, chain 2, 2dc, in each chain 2 corner sp. Dc in each sc across. Repeat that around. Join with a slip stitch to the top of chain 3. Fasten off the pink cotton.

Round 3: Join the white in the same stitch as the slip stitch. Chain one. Sc in each next dc. 2sc, chain 1, 2sc in next chain 2 corner sp. Sc in each dc across. 2sc, chain 1, 2 sc in the next chain 2 corner sp. Sc in each dc across. Repeat that around. Join with a slip stitch into chain 1. Fasten off and then weave all the ends into the back of the work to finish.

Let's move on now to some more advanced patterns.

Curtains from Heaven

Use a color of acrylic yarn that goes with your décor.

Measure the length of the curtains you have now, and cast on enough stitches to equal that amount. Single crochet across, then chain 3 when you reach the other end. Chain 3, skip 2, and triple crochet across the row.

Repeat this pattern so you have a very open work panel, then fold over the top section so you have a tunnel that is 3 inches thick. Sew it down, and tie off. Slide the curtain rod in this tunnel, and your curtains are ready to go!

Grandmother's Apron

Cotton yarn works well for aprons, but you can use acrylic if you like.

Cast on 25, and single crochet across the row. Turn, and single crochet back across the other side. Repeat this until you have a panel that is 2 feet thick. Decrease as you move up the neck until you are happy with the width, then tie off. Crochet chains for the neck and the ties, and attach. Tie off, and your apron is ready!

End Table Covers

Use a light, thin yarn for this one

Cast on 40. Single crochet across, then join the ends. Working inside the project, alternate using triple crochet and double crochet, and stitching in every other stitch.

Once you reach the center, tie off the end of it and work in the ends.

Chapter 7 – Making Your Own Patterns

If you have crocheted much in the past, or if you are any good at crochet, you will know that there are all kinds of patterns that are in your head, just waiting to get out. You don't have to be super skilled at this to be able to make your own patterns, you just have to know how to do certain stitches, and have the imagination to make those stitches into patterns.

You don't have to write down those patterns, or you can if you want to know how you did it if you ever want to do it again. Either way, you know that you have the freedom to make these your own, and all you have to do if you want your own new project is pick out what color yarn you want to use, and you are set.

There is so much freedom in this, you will be amazed at just how easy it is to make things your own. Don't get discouraged if it takes you a while to decide what to make, or if you need to try a few times to get what you want. This is a project that is meant to be personal, so do what you need to do to make it your own.

No matter what, there is no hurry to getting these done, as long as you are having fun doing it. Follow these patterns as guides to know what you are making, but feel free to make them your own any way that you can. If you like, you can also use these patterns as inspiration to make your own crafts. This is such a freeing craft, all you need to do is decide how you want it, and you can have it that way.

We used acrylic on all of these patterns, but you are free to use your own size and color… make it unique!

Super Scarf

Wool is great for winter, sport weight for summer.

Measure the length that you would like your scarf to be, then cast on that many stitches. Holding a length of fun fir to your yarn of choice, single crochet across the row.

Chain 1, turn, and single crochet back across. Repeat this pattern until you are happy with the thickness of your scarf. Record what you do.

Afghan for your Soul

Scrap yarn works great for this pattern.

Cast on 145. Double crochet from the beginning, all the way across your row. Chain 3, then triple crochet back across. Chain 2, then double crochet across the row again. Chain 1, then single crochet.

Repeat this 3 row pattern until you are happy with the length of your afghan. Tie off and crochet a border around the edge. Tie off.

Happy Handbag

Use bamboo for the body, and fun fir around the top for a flirty appeal

Cast on 20, then single crochet one row. Chain 1, turn, and double crochet in the next 2 stitches. Single crochet in the next stitch, then double crochet in the next 2. Repeat this pattern across the row.

Chain 1, turn, and work the same pattern across the row to the other side. Keep working this pattern, you will notice that you get some nice texture with your handbag as you do, then tie off when you have a rectangle that is twice as long as it is wide.

Fold your rectangle in half, sew up the open sides, and crochet 2 rows of fun fir around the top. Crochet a small strip out of fun fir for the sides, then sew the strap on for a handle.

Make sure everything is secure, and you are good to go!

The Date Night Handbag

Use a flashy little yarn for this one.

Holding a length of fun fir to acrylic, cast on 25. Single crochet with both yarns across the row, then chain 2. Double crochet back across the row. Make a handbag as big as you prefer them to be, then fold it in half.

Sew up two sides of the bag, then tie off. Crochet another strip for the handle, and sew that to your bag. Tie off and show off.

Fabulous Throws

Use a sport weight yarn for this one, fun fir will add a bit of shine.

Cast on 75, then single crochet across the tow. Chain 3, then triple crochet in each stitch back across. Chain 3, turn, and repeat. Move across the rows, repeating this pattern, until you are happy with the size of your throw.

Crochet a border to your throw, and tie it off securely.

Puffy Pillows

Use a multi-colored acrylic yarn for these.

Cast on 35, then single crochet across. Chain 1, then triple crochet 3 times in the next stitch. Single crochet in the next 2 stitches, then triple crochet in the next stitch.

Repeat this pattern all the way across the row. To start row 2, chain 1, then single crochet in the next 2 stitches. Chain 3, then triple crochet in the next stitch. Single crochet in the next 2 stitches, then triple crochet in the next stitch.

Repeat this pattern all the way across the row. Alternate rows 1 and 2 until you have a puffy square panel. Tie off and repeat for the other side.

Sew both panels together, stuff well, then sew the rest of the way closed. Add a long fringe to the border and tie off.

Conclusion

Tunisian crochet is unique, it may look complicated but it is very simple learn. This book has provided all of the skills needed to begin the hobby of Tunisian crochet. Learning more advanced techniques will give all of your crochet projects a polished look but the simple Tunisian stitch is enough to create anything you can imagine.

This new found skill is sure to make you happy when you finish your first handmade scarf or wrist warmers. Make sure you keep enough yarn on hand, nothing is worse than starting a project and having to stop before it is finished because you ran out of yarn. Try different gauge hooks to broaden your skill base and different yarn thickness to personalize the item.

Although everyone has seen those odd long crochet hooks next to the familiar ones in the craft stores, most people do not know how to use them. After reading this book, anyone can use the Afghan hook to work up some warm, cozy, fabric for cold winter nights, or a new trendy cell phone holder.

Tunisian crochet never gets boring. There are always new colors, new patterns, and new skills to choose and learn. It is easy to keep things fresh, just change up the yarn colors or learn a new stitch. Yarn is available in so many textures, thickness, and styles you can use one pattern and create several different looking results.

Blankets and other items will need to be washed and cared for. Information on how to care for each style or brand of yarn is on the yarn packaging. Always follow the yarn manufactures care instructions to keep your items looking their best.

Tunisian crochet works great on large projects and small projects because the stitches are tight and uniform. These stitches work great for items like cat toys, dog toys, and for making all sorts of soft toys for babies and young children. Patterns for toys and other fun stuff are available on line in e-books and on blogs.

Always save the left over yarn, there are always new and exciting projects to tackle with yarn scraps. Scraps are great for granny squares and granny squares are great for blankets. It is a good idea to package up yarn scraps and keep them in a plastic container or bag to keep them clean and ready to use.

Now you have ten items that you can create and enjoy. They may end up finding a new home when birthdays and holidays come around. Once you are hooked it is difficult to stop crocheting. It is ok though, everyone wants something homemade and those projects you completed will find new homes quickly.

Made in the USA
Las Vegas, NV
27 January 2022

42396004R00056